Praise for Frankie, the Walk 'N Roll Therapy Dog Visits Libby's House

Barbara Techel takes us beyond our human reasoning and limited sight by engaging our imaginations grounded in truth through the eyes of her little dog Frankie - who doesn't allow her physical challenges to limit her purpose or her gift of healing to all those who come into contact with her. Into Libby's House we ___ ce and charm only a little dog in wheels can claim with unabashed healing love for tl ___ body.

~ Dr. Kim Bloomer, veterinary naturopath, au ___ turally, www.animaltalknaturally.com

Frankie's heart-warming story signifies the therapeutic bond created between animals, disabled individuals, and older adults, as Barbara respectfully reaches out to a population that goes unnoticed at times. Again, the author has done a brilliant job to include real lessons, diversity, and a positive sense of awareness all inside a children's book. Grandparents must read this story with their grandchildren. The talking points for a parent and child are so delicately presented during Frankie's journey, you can't help but feel like your eyes have been opened to the important things in life. Bravo you two! You have written a story that needed to be told!

~Melissa M. Williams, author of the Iggy the Iguana Series, www.iggytheiguana.com

This wonderful story creatively introduces children to therapy dog service through the eyes of Frankie, a special dachshund with mobility impairment. But adversity does not stop Frankie and Barbara from making a positive difference in the lives of the elderly by bringing love and comfort to their assisted living facility. A superb job of expressing a realistic view of life and issues for the elderly in assisted living, as well as introducing the numerous contexts in which dogs and their humans can be of service as therapy dog teams. Valuable lessons of patience, listening, and understanding are demonstrated in a story children will easily relate to.

~Dawn Kairns, author of *Maggie, the dog who changed my life*, www.dawnkairns.com

This new book about Frankie, the walk 'n roll dog, takes young readers on another inspiring journey. It reaches past ice cream, candy and balloons, giving children more understanding and appreciation about life. In this second book in the series, Frankie becomes a therapy dog and brings healing love to old people. All children who have read the first book relate to Frankie's courage. Now, they will be fascinated by her ability to open the hearts of old people and bring hope and friendship into their lives. This is a wonderful story of the human canine bond for children, parents, and grandparents. Barbara has performed an important service in writing a book that will find a wide audience for kids and take them into the world of senior citizens. It will help ease the transition of understanding, acceptance and caring. This is a children's non-fiction book with real substance… done with a gentle touch that kids can relate to.

~Robert McCarty, author of the series Planet of the Dogs, www.planetofthedogs.net

In *Frankie, the Walk 'N Roll Therapy Dog Visits Libby's House*, Barbara and Frankie share important messages about physical and mental infirmities and some of the changes we'll go through as we get older. This book will help both children and adults learn how to better interact with people of different abilities and accept the changes as people get older. I love the bond between Barbara and Frankie and the way that Barbara explains things to Frankie as they go about their visit. The example of missing a friend who passes on, while also making new friends, is important. Go Barbara and Frankie! You truly are on a roll!

~Jenny Pavlovic, author of *8 State Hurricane Kate*, www.8statekate.net

All one needs to do is see the expression in the eyes of those Frankie touches to know she is tangible love. When the body fails, the spirit soars! Frankie's visits along with Barb's gentle nature are a true blessing to Libby's house.

~Christine Thill, RN Administrator of Libby's House
www.libbyshouse.com

In *Frankie, The Walk 'N Roll Therapy Dog Visits Libby's House*, Barbara Techel shares the heartwarming story about how one small dog with a huge heart brings joy, affection and comfort to nursing home residents. Frankie's exuberant spirit and refusal to let her disability slow her down are an inspiration to anyone facing challenges and provide hope that anything is possible.

~Ingrid King, author of *Buckley's Story – Lessons from a Feline Master Teacher*
www.pethealing.net

Once again, Frankie is here to inspire us and share her wonderful view of the world on two wheels. Barbara Techel's loving story is filled with valuable information about what it takes to become a therapy dog and the joy it can bring to others in need. This is a great book for children to learn how each one of us, no matter how small or different, can bring joy to the life of others. A beautiful and important story for all ages!

~Rain Fordyce, inspirational life coach and author of *I am Learning All the Time*
www.homeschooladventurebooks.com

Reading Barbara Techel's dog book series is like stepping into a world of tenderness and compassion. Frankie will tickle your funny bone and pull at your heartstrings. Children and adults alike will fully enjoy this warm and utterly inspiring story about a brave little therapy dog and how she changes people's lives.

~Mayra Calvani, Midwest Book Review, www.midwestbookreview.com

Frankie, the Walk 'N Roll Therapy Dog Visits Libby's House is a testament to how much impact animals can have on human lives. Frankie is a beautiful example of unconditional love wrapped in a body filled with joy. Barbara's willingness and sensitivity to addressing deep subjects surrounding life challenges is a gift to all humankind. She and Frankie are two blessed reminders that each day is a gift.

~Sage Lewis, Animal and Human Whisperer, Author of *JAVA: The True Story of a Shelter Dog Who Rescued a Woman*, www.DancingPorcupine.com

Frankie

the walk 'n roll therapy dog visits libby's house

To: Elkhart Lake Elementary School - you make a difference and keep on rolling!

Barbara Gaschel &

Frankie

Frankie

the walk 'n roll therapy dog visits libby's house

by barbara gail techel
illustrations by victoria kay lieffring

joyful paw prints

wisconsin

joyful paw prints

wisconsin

Dedicated to grandparents everywhere who share with us their wisdom, their grace, and endearing love; and to my sweet Frankie, who continues to enrich my journey beyond anything I could have ever imagined.

2009 Wisconsin Pet Hall of Fame Companion

INDRODUCTION

Sometimes life throws us a curve ball. That does not mean we should give up on our dreams. It just means we have to look at things in a new way.

Right when I had my life all planned out, my dachshund Frankie suffered a spinal cord injury and became paralyzed. Six months before that, I had brought home a yellow lab puppy. I named her Kylie. It was my plan to train Kylie to become a therapy dog, so I took her to puppy classes and then to obedience training. Our next step would be to take the required therapy dog test.

I had to put the testing with Kylie on hold because Frankie required special care due to her paralysis. I devoted much of my time doing physical therapy for Frankie in hopes that she would walk again. After three months, I was told statistically that most likely she would not regain full use of her back legs.

In July 2006, Frankie was custom-fitted for a dog cart, which is similar to a wheelchair for people. She amazes me every day with her positive attitude. Nothing stops her from living a full, happy life. Frankie loves walking in the woods showing off her superb hunting skills by sniffing out chipmunks and squirrels. She is still the best doorbell we could ask for. She alerts us with loud barks as she speeds to the front door. Best of all, she is a loving companion. Every chance she gets, she enjoys nestling in my lap.

Realizing the lessons she taught me because of her fighting spirit, I wrote her story in *Frankie, the Walk 'N Roll Dog,* which I published in 2008, so I could share her inspirational message with children. Visiting with kids was a natural for Frankie, and one day it struck me out of the blue! I thought to myself, maybe Frankie was meant to be my therapy dog. Maybe we could become a registered team and visit nursing homes and patients in hospitals and bring smiles and joy to even more people. That is when we met a very special teacher named Julie. She is a tester with Therapy Dogs, Inc. and she encouraged us to become a team.

This book, *Frankie, the Walk 'N Roll Therapy Dog Visits Libby's House* is the story of some of Frankie's work as a therapy dog and the difference she is making in the lives of the elderly. The story is told by Frankie herself, with a little help from me, her proud and grateful mom.

WHAT IS A THERAPY DOG?

Definition as stated by Wikepedia:

"A therapy dog is a dog trained to provide affection and comfort to people in hospitals, retirement homes, nursing homes, mental institutions, schools, and stressful situations such as disaster areas.

Therapy dogs come in all sizes and breeds. The most important characteristic of a therapy dog is its temperament. A good therapy dog must be friendly, patient, confident, at ease in all situations, and gentle. Therapy dogs must enjoy human contact and be content to be petted and handled, sometimes clumsily.

A therapy dog's primary job is to allow unfamiliar people to make physical contact with it and to enjoy that contact. Children in particular enjoy hugging animals; adults usually enjoy simply petting the dog. The dog might need to be lifted onto, or climb onto, an invalid's lap or bed and sit or lie comfortably there. Many dogs contribute to the visiting experience by performing small tricks for their audiences or by playing carefully structured games."

In addition, I would like to say that therapy dogs are benefiting hospice patients, as well as children struggling with physical challenges.

I hear water running in the kitchen sink. I know what that means!

"Time for your bath, Frankie." Mom gently takes me out of my wheelchair. "But first you have to go potty." Mom helps me go potty on the toilet because I cannot feel when I have to go. I had an accident and I am partially paralyzed. This means I don't have any feeling in my back legs, so it makes it difficult for me to walk without the help of my wheelchair.

"Good girl, Frankie!" Mom is always proud of me.

She hands me over to my papa. "Here you go, Papa. Frankie is ready for her bath."

He gently places me in the kitchen sink, and uses the sprayer to wet my silky, red fur. The warm water feels soothing as it glides down my back. I balance my tiny paws on the edge of the sink and drift into a sleepy state as Papa lathers me with lots of soapy suds. "Ahhhhh…."

"Time for the final rinse, Frankie." Papa startled me and interrupted my spa treatment as he whisks the suds away. I watch them swish and swirl down the drain. Papa wraps me in a warm, fluffy towel. "Come on, little one. Let's cuddle until you are dry." He sits in his favorite chair and puts me in his lap. I close my eyes and thank my lucky stars for snuggle time with my papa.

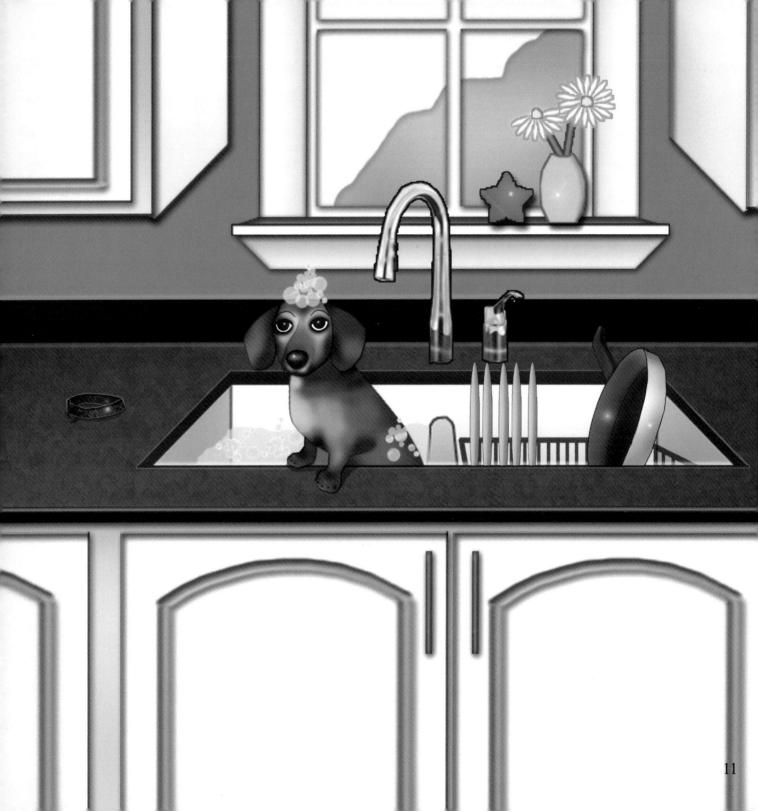

I have to be squeaky clean and well groomed to be a therapy dog. I remember when my mom was training my Labrador sister, Kylie, to do therapy work. Mom dreamed of taking Kylie to nursing homes and bringing happiness to the residents. But, that was put on hold when I became paralyzed and Mom had to take care of me.

A year later I was healed, so Mom and I began to visit schools in nearby cities. Now, we share my remarkable story of living life to the fullest in a wheelchair. We teach children that every challenge can be overcome by having a positive attitude.

One day, Mom and I met an exceptional elementary school teacher named Julie when we visited her classroom. As Mom was getting ready for our presentation, Julie said, "My dog, Preston, is a therapy dog. He comes to school with me every Wednesday and the children take turns reading to him. It helps them concentrate and it enhances their reading skills."

My mom's face lit up. "I have always dreamed of doing therapy dog work with Kylie," she said. "But, I put my dream on hold when Frankie got hurt."

Aa Bb Cc Dd Ee Ff Gg Hh Ii Jj Kk Ll Mr

After the presentation, Mom was packing up and Julie was putting the desks back in rows. "I think Frankie would make a wonderful therapy dog," Julie said. "She is so well-behaved with the children."

Mom looked at Julie sadly. "I'm nervous Frankie wouldn't pass the required testing," Mom said. "She's never had any formal obedience training." Julie smiled. "I happen to be a tester with Therapy Dogs Incorporated. I would be happy to meet with both of you and go over the test so you would feel more comfortable. I think you and Frankie would have no problem passing the test. Frankie is a natural!"

Mom's eyes filled with tears. "You really think so?" Julie nodded. Mom knelt next to me. "What do you think Frankie?" she asked. "Can we do it?"

I looked up to her and blinked my fawn-like eyes.

On a cool, windy afternoon, Julie came to our house to help Mom and me practice for the test.

"You and Frankie must walk together as a team with Frankie at your side. First, walk slowly, then quickly, and then turn around and walk back to me."

Mom held my leash and I pranced beside her as we made our way into the backyard. Every now and then, I would look up at her to see if I was doing it right.

"Good job, Frankie!" Julie grinned from ear to ear. "Second, Frankie will need to accept strangers petting her all over."

I sat contently while Julie stroked my head, body, tail, tummy, and paws. Mmmmm, I liked that test!

"The next test is a hard one, but a very important one," Julie explained. "Frankie cannot be afraid around wheelchairs. We will have to wait to practice until we visit a nursing home, which we will do soon."

Mom grinned. "I have a feeling Frankie will pass that test with flying colors!"

birds
welcome

"Now, for the next test," Julie said. "She cannot be aggressive toward another dog. Wait here." Julie walked to her car as Mom and I sat on the lawn. Julie returned with her dog, Preston. I stood erect on my front paws as Preston came closer.

"Woof! Woof! Woof!" I let him know this was my yard and my mom.

We met nose to nose and sniffed each other. Then, I twirled around in my cart to show him how it works. Mom and Julie giggled as Preston flopped down on his side.

"The last test requires that you and Frankie be well groomed when you make your therapy dog visits."

Mom laughed loudly. "No problem. Frankie loves bath time!"

Julie smiled widely. "You both did very well and will make a great team."

Hot-diggity dog! I passed all the initial tests. Mom swept me into her arms and gave me a big hug.

Three weeks later, Mom and I met Julie and Preston outside a nursing home. Preston and I sniffed each other while Mom gave Julie a big hug.

Julie looked down at me. "This is the day I will see how you react around wheelchairs, Frankie," she said. "We will also need to see how well you interact with everyone. So, if you are ready, let's go in."

I rolled happily through the front doors. The receptionist and director of the nursing home were waiting for us.

"Welcome! We are so happy you are here." The receptionist bent down and patted the top of my head. "You are the sweetest little thing!" she said.

All of a sudden I heard a familiar noise. I spun around and couldn't believe my eyes! Birds of bright yellow, baby blue, and cocoa brown were flitting from branch to branch within a big glass container. I scurried up to the front and pressed my nose against the glass. The birds scolded me, "Tweet! Tweet! Tweet!"

I paced back and forth wishing with all my might I could get inside and catch a bird. Mom looked at me sternly. "Now, Frankie, that is enough. You are frightening those poor birds. It is time to do our therapy dog visit and you must behave."

I looked at Preston and Julie. They were waiting for me, so I walked nicely over to join them. Then, we all got on the elevator and went to the fourth floor where the residents live.

As we strolled off the elevator, a man in a wheelchair came rolling toward us. "Oh, what do we have here?" He reached down and stroked my fur. "You have wheels just like me, little pup. What happened?"

My mom told the kind man how I hurt my back and how my dog cart helps me walk. His eyes fill with tears. "That is so wonderful! How nice of you to come here to visit," he said. "You just made my day!"

Preston and I brought many smiles to everyone that day as we made our way through the hallways to visit with all the residents and staff.

A nurse giggled when she saw us. "Can I pet your dogs?"

Julie grinned. "Yes, please do. That is why we are here."

After an hour of visiting, I started to slow down. I was ready for my nap.

"I think Frankie has had enough for today, Julie," Mom explained.

We made our way back to the elevator and rode down to the first floor. We walked out of the building and into the fresh air and sat down on the front lawn. Julie handed my mom a signed certificate. "I'm so happy to tell you both that you have passed the final test," she said. "I'm so proud of you, Frankie. You will bring so much joy to many people with your therapy dog visits."

One blustery afternoon, I was curled in the front of the warm, gas stove when I heard Mom talking to someone named Patty. "We would love to visit your facility. Frankie and I will be there every third Monday of the month at one o'clock in the afternoon."

Just as I drifted back to sleep, my mom startled me. "Oh Frankie, guess what?" she said, "We will start our therapy dog work next week on Monday. We will visit a very special place called Libby's House."

Libby's House is a senior assisted living facility. It is kind of like a big house where many older people live together. There are many people who work at Libby's House to help the residents. There are nurses, cleaning staff, cooks, and activity directors. It will be a special day when we make our first visit.

The big day has finally arrived! I know this because Mom is loading my wheelchair into the car. Mom scoops me up. "Time to buckle you into your doggie car seat, my little Frankie." I perch my feet on the end and get into position as the official co-pilot for our ride into town.

"Ready? Set? Here we go, Frankie," Mom says excitedly. "We are off to Libby's House to bring smiles to the residents."

Mom pulls up to a big tan house with brown shutters and many windows. Birds are chirping loudly as they sit perched on several bird feeders in the yard.

My mom takes me out of the car and puts me into my wheelchair. "Time to make new friends, Frankie," Mom says.

As we roll through the first set of doors, we have to stop. My mom presses a button that looks like a doorbell, but I don't hear it ring so I don't bark. Patty, the activity director, comes to the door and punches a code in the keypad on the wall. The door opens.

"Welcome to Libby's House," Patty says. "We are thrilled you are here!"

"We are happy to visit you," Mom replies.

"Everyone finishes lunch around one o'clock," Patty says as we pass the cafeteria. I try to snatch up a few leftover crumbs on the floor, but my mom tugs at my leash. Drats! "Let me show you where they will gather after they are done eating." We follow Patty into a large room with a couch, lots of chairs, and a big screen TV. There are patio doors that open into

A man sitting in the recliner notices me and smiles the biggest smile I have ever seen. "What do we have here?" he says. "I adore dogs!"

"This is Frankie," Patty says as she winks at Daniel. "I have a feeling you two will become friends fast."

I overhear Patty telling my mom that Daniel is in his early seventies. But, that does not stop him from getting down on his hands and knees to pet me. Daniel gives me a big hug and kisses the top of my head. "You are the cutest little dog I have ever seen," he says.

Mom hands Daniel my pink leash. "Would you like to take Frankie for a little walk?"

Daniel nods enthusiastically as he takes my leash. He seems to have an extra bounce in his step as we jubilantly move down the hallway.

A few moments later, we return to the living room and Daniel eases his way onto the couch.

Mom says, "Would you like Frankie to sit on your lap, Daniel?"

"You bet I would."

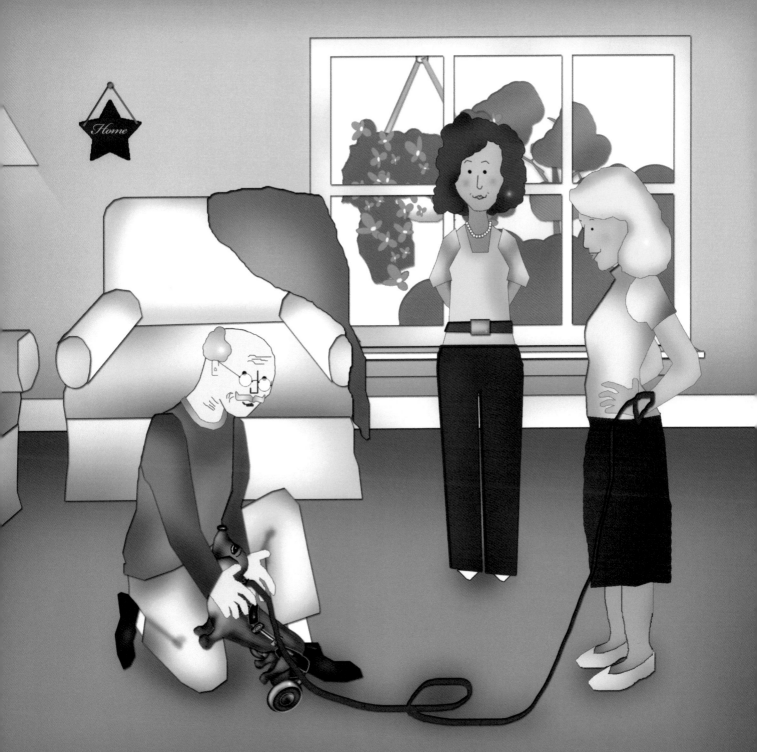

Mom lifts me onto Daniel's lap. "You are so special, Frankie," he says. I look up at him and notice his eyes are filling with tears. "I feel so sorry for her," Daniel says sadly.

"You don't need to feel sorry for Frankie," Mom says. "Visiting you makes her very happy."

"It does?" Daniel holds me close. "Frankie is perfect, unlike me. I am not perfect," Daniel's voice cracks.

"We think you are perfect just the way you are." My mom tries to reassure Daniel. I rest my head on his knee and raise my eyebrows. Daniel smiles and his whole face lights up.

The nurse comes into the room. "Time to take your medication, Daniel," she says. She holds his arm and helps him up from the couch. He glances down at me one more time. "Please come visit me again, Frankie."

"Arf!" I let out a soft bark as the nurse and Daniel walk to the kitchen.

My mom and Patty sit down. "Daniel used to be a policeman and was a crime scene investigator," Patty says. "Most days he sits in his room listening to the radio. Daniel loves to sing." Patty and my mom both smile.

Many of the residents at Libby's house sometimes can't remember things. The staff helps them remember when to take their medicine, when to eat, and when to go to bed at night. It is kind of like being a kid again like when your mom and dad had to help you with those things.

Spending time at Libby's House with Daniel makes my heart feel all warm and fuzzy inside. Sometimes older people feel lonely. When I visit, they share stories about their younger years and talk about when they had a pet. They also enjoy throwing my ball for me and feeding me treats.

The activity directors plan many special activities for the residents. On Tuesday afternoons, they all gather in the music room. A resident or staff member plays the piano and everyone sings songs from the old days. The whole time the music plays, Daniel smiles. He can't always remember the words, but he hums along to the tune.

They also celebrate special birthdays at Libby's House. Today is Martha's birthday. She is turning one hundred years old! Martha and I have something in common. She is in a wheelchair just like me.

There are colorful tablecloths on each table in celebration of her birthday. There are also balloons tied to each chair. The balloons are canary yellow, petunia pink, and sea green. A birthday cake with white frosting and sprinkles of jazzy confetti is on the table in front of Martha.

The cook says loudly, "One hundred candles would have never fit on your cake Martha, so I put one big candle in the center to represent your 100 years."

"Good thing! You might have burned down the building lighting one hundred candles!" Martha giggles.

Martha's family has come from far and wide to be with her. Martha's 75-year old daughter, Sara, is sitting next to her. "How does it feel to turn 100 years old, Mother?"

Martha thinks for a moment. "I'm not as agile as I used to be, but I'm happy to be alive to see the sunshine and my

I love spending time with each resident when I visit. Sometimes we all gather in the living room and my mom reads them my story from my first book, Frankie, the Walk 'N Roll Dog. This helps them understand how I hurt myself and why I am in a doggie wheelchair.

I remember another day when we were at Libby's house. My mom was all done reading when Ted said, "What happened to Frankie that she has to be in a wheelchair?" Mom smiled and again told Ted why. Sometimes older people can't remember for very long. Mom whispers softly to me, "Frankie, we just have to be patient and help them remember."

After Martha and her guests have cake, Mom talks to the residents. "In Germany, where the dachshund originated, a nickname for Frankie's breed is known as Teckel, spelled T-E-C-K-E-L," Mom says. "The funny thing is my last name is Techel, though I spell it T-E-C-H-E-L. So, everywhere we visit, I tell everyone we are the Techel-Teckel team!"

Everyone smiles.

Edith says, "I used to have a dog that looked just like you, Frankie. His name was Schutzie." She pretends to roll something in her hands and explains, "Every evening I would give Schutzie a special treat of cooked ground beef for dinner." Her eyes get a little misty. "Schutzie would always sit with me in my recliner every night while I read the paper. When it was time for bed, he would follow me, jump on the bed, and wait for me to take off my slippers. Then, he would lay next to me with his head on the pillow, and I would cover him with the blanket."

Even though Mom and I heard this same story last time when we visited, we sit politely and listen again. We pretend it is the first time we heard her story. Edith smiles and is happy that we pay attention.

Janice is another resident at Libby's house. When she sees me she says, "I don't like dogs."

"That's okay Janice, I understand if you don't like dogs," Mom says. "How come you don't like dogs?"

"I was bit by one when I was a young girl," Janice explains.

"I would be afraid, too, if that happened to me," my mom says sympathetically.

Janice grins. "I don't like cats either, and I don't like fish."

Mom laughs.

Eva, another resident at Libby's House, wanders into the room. She is carrying a large, stuffed green bag in one hand, and her purse is clutched in her other hand.

"What do you have in the bag, Eva?" my mom says.

Eva rummages through the bag. "This is material I will use to make a coat for my snowman," she says as she pulls out an oversized puffy snowman and sits him on the couch next to her. Then, she pulls out orange and black plaid material. "This is left over from a Halloween costume I made for Billy last month."

I tilt my head to the side and look at my mom. Who could Billy be?

Eva gets up abruptly and heads to the kitchen.

"Who is Billy?" Mom asks Patty.

"Billy is Eva's 55-year old son."

I am not quite sure I understand why Eva would make a Halloween costume for her adult son. Then, my mom says, "Oh, I see. Eva is reminiscing." Mom and Patty smile at each other.

My mom likes to dress me as a hot dog on Halloween, complete with fake ketchup, mustard, and relish. I don't think that is particularly funny, but I go along with it because I love her.

"Well, Frankie," my mom says. "I think we should head back home."

Noooo. I don't want to leave. I plant my front feet firmly in place and hold tight to the ground. I won't budge as my Mom tries to pull me along at the end of my leash.

"Come on, Frankie." Mom giggles as she tugs a little harder. "We will visit again next month," she says.

We will? Yippee! Okay, now I am happy to go. I know I will see everyone again, so I roll happily to the front door.

It's one month later. Mom puts a big yellow happy face on the calendar and says, "Today is a special day, Frankie. We're going back to Libby's House."

"Arf!" I tell her. I wish I could wag my tail because that's the way dogs say they are happy, but my tail doesn't work.

Mom puts me in my doggie car seat and away we go. The sun feels especially warm today as we drive to Libby's House. The grass is getting greener by the day and tiny buds are popping from the tree branches.

April

Sunday	Monday	Tuesday	Wednesday	Thursday	Friday	Saturday
			1	2	3	4
5	6	7	8	9	10	11
12	13	14	15	16	17	18
19	20	21	22	23	24	25
26	27	28	29	30		

treats

food

food

www.JOYFULPAWS.com

FRANKIE

The Walk 'N Roll Dog

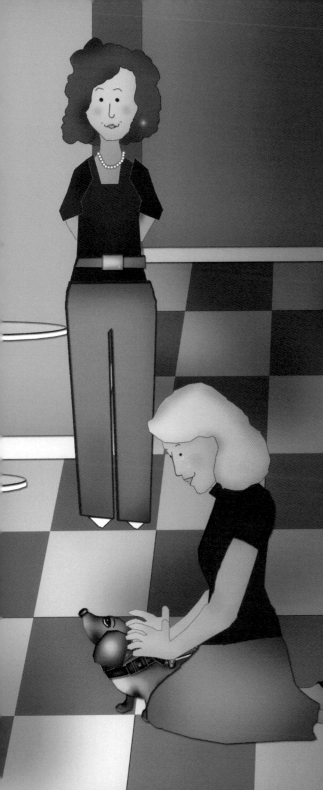

I roll happily through the front doors of Libby's house, eager to see my best pal, Daniel. I look into the big living room, but do not see him in the chair where he is normally waiting to greet me. I look around the room but he is nowhere to be found.

"Let's go see if Daniel is in his room today, Frankie," Mom says.

We quickly walk to his room and peek in. Something is different. I don't hear the radio playing. The stacks of books on the end table are no longer there. The large stuffed yellow Labrador toy that is always on his bed is gone, too.

I look up to my mom and wonder, where could Daniel be today?

Just as we start to turn around, Patty, the activity director, comes into the room. Her eyes fill with tears. "I'm sorry to have to tell you this," she said, "but Daniel died on Friday."

My mom starts to cry softly. She bends down and takes me out of my wheelchair and hugs me close.

Patty pats my head and says, "Daniel loved you so much, Frankie. You always made his day when you visited. Thank you for being his friend."

The following month flowers are blooming with every color in the rainbow and people are outside cutting their grass. Kids are playing in the park. The warm wind blows my ears back as we drive to Libby's house.

It is hard to know I won't see Daniel anymore when I visit. But, I hold my head high as I roll through the front doors once again.

Patty is waiting for us. She bends down to stroke my fur. "Frankie, there is someone new waiting to meet you," she says happily.

"Her name is Lyla, and she loves dogs. I have told her all about you, and she is eager to visit with you." Patty leads the way as Mom and I walk side by side.

Lyla is sitting in the chair where Daniel used to wait for me. Her hair is short and silver and her walker is resting next to the chair.

Patty quietly says to my mom, "It is hard to understand Lyla when she talks, but she tries to communicate."

Mom picks me up and kneels down in front of Lyla. She rests the front of my paws on the arm of the chair while she holds the back of my wheelchair in her hands. Lyla's hands are shaking as she reaches out to pet my head. She looks deep into my eyes and chatters up a storm. I am not sure what she is saying, but my heart feels all warm and fuzzy again. I have made another new friend.

After visiting with Lyla, I make my rounds to each resident so they can pet me. An hour later my mom says, "I think it is time to head home, Frankie."

I lift my ears and jump to my feet. Mom says goodbye to everyone. They all wave as we walk out to the car.

Mom pats my chest as she straps me into my doggie car seat. "For a little dog, you have the biggest heart ever, Frankie."

As Mom starts the engine, she reaches over, smiles, and puts her arm around me. "I'm so proud of you, Frankie. Thank you for being my therapy dog and making a positive difference in the world."

I slowly blink my eyes and drift off to sleep as we ride home.

Acknowledgements

This book may not have been written if I had not met the sweet man I refer to in the book as Daniel. I felt a little out of my comfort zone when first visiting Libby's House, partly because I was hoping Frankie and I would make a difference. Meeting Daniel for the first time, seeing the exuberant joy on his face, and his instant connection with Frankie, affirmed for me that my heart had led me to the right place. Daniel was my guide as I wrote this book. Thank you, Daniel, for teaching me that each of us can truly can make a difference. You will always have a special place in my heart.

This amazing journey would not be possible without Frankie, my little dog on wheels. Not a day goes by that I don't thank God for the gift of you and all the beautiful lessons of life you continue to teach me. You continue to guide me just by being the joyful spirit that you are. You are my biggest inspiration.

To my husband John: what can I say that I have not already said? Your support of my dreams and hopes is a gift I am so grateful for. Without your love for me, I could not continue to follow this path. You are simply the best.

To my biggest fan, my mom: not everyone is lucky enough to say that their mom is their biggest fan, but you, my dear mom, continue to rejoice in each step of my path, encourage me when I feel lost, and love me no matter what. Thank you for your unconditional love that continues to inspire me to be the best me.

To Julie Hauck, one the most genuine, kind people on this earth: there is no doubt the reason why we met. Your gentle, sweet nature calmed my fears and helped me see that Frankie and I could indeed become a therapy dog team. Your gift of believing in us continues to bring me joy each and every time I do volunteer work with Frankie. I can never thank you enough.

To my illustrator, Victoria Kay Lieffring: thank you for once again understanding my vision for Frankie's message, for bringing my words to life with your endearing illustrations, and for continuing to grow along with me on this journey.

A big heartfelt thank you to my editor, Yvonne Perry (www.wrtitersinthesky.com): thank you for introducing me to the "think tank" during the editing of this book. It was a challenge I welcomed, grew, and learned from. Your love for Frankie's mission makes my heart rejoice. I'm so grateful our paths crossed.

To Christine Thill, RN and owner of Libby's House (www.libbyshouse.com): thank you for welcoming Frankie and me with open arms to your beautiful facility. Being a part of your mission of "providing peace of mind to the residents by offering dignified care," has opened my eyes and heart to a new appreciation for life. Each time we visit, I leave with a feeling of fulfillment I find hard to describe in words.

Thank you to Jessica Dockter, graphic designer (www.leedesign.org), who brings all the illustrations, words, and pages together to make a wonderful book. Thank you for always taking on my challenges with a smile, and understanding that my books are my heart.

To my family, friends and fans of Frankie who kept asking, "When is the next book coming out?" Thank you for believing in us and for supporting my heart's calling. Your kindness means the world to me.

To the staff and residents of Libby's House, it is so rewarding to know each of you. Your friendships fill my heart with joy each time we visit. Of course, the names of Libby's House residents have been changed to protect their privacy.

Barbara is the author of the multi-award winning book, Frankie, the Walk 'N Roll Dog. When her dachshund, Frankie, suffered a spinal injury, Barbara had her custom-fitted for a wheelchair. Frankie persevered, and Barbara realized the beautiful opportunity she had to share Frankie and give others hope and inspiration to be the best they can be. Along with sharing Frankie's story with children, Barbara and Frankie routinely volunteer as a therapy dog team at local hospitals, nursing homes, and hospice centers, spreading joy wherever they go.

Since 2005, Barbara has been a contributing writer for the Depot Dispatch sharing stories of her animals, as well as other furry friends she has met along the way. In 2006, Barbara's article, "Cassie and Frankie Inspire a Writer," won honorable mention from bestselling authors, Linda and Allen Anderson of Angel Animals Network.

Barbara hopes Frankie's story as a therapy dog will teach that no matter what life challenges we face, we can still give back to the world. She also hopes it will encourage children to spend quality time with their grandparents and cherish each and every moment.

Barbara lives in the Midwest with her husband, John; Frankie, the walk 'n roll dog; and Kylie, a yellow English Labrador.

You can read more about Barbara at www.joyfulpaws.com or Frankie at www.frankiethewalknrolldog.blogspot.com

Freelance designer Victoria Kay Lieffring graduated in 2006 from the Milwaukee Institute of Art & Design with a bachelor of fine arts degree in interior architecture and design. Currently working at the Kohler Company, she renders the designs for the structure and display of the company's tradeshow booths.

She enjoys acrylic painting, sculpting, and watercolors, and takes pleasure in her creative work as a graphic designer. The Elkhart Lake, Wisconsin native served as the illustrator for Frankie, the Walk'N Roll Dog and Frankie, the Walk'N Roll Therapy Dog Visits Libby's House.

Other books by Barbara Techel

Frankie, the Walk 'N Roll Dog

Frankie, the Walk 'N Roll Dog Activity Book

To purchase copies of Frankie's books please visit
www.joyfulpaws.com.

To keep up to date on Frankie's adventures you can follow her on her blog at
www.frankiethewalknrolldog.blogspot.com

Follow me on Twitter
www.twitter.com/walknrolldog

CPSIA information can be obtained
at www.ICGtesting.com
Printed in the USA
253710LV00002B